Growing Up With Music

The Amazing Marsalis Family

By Catherine Murphy

Contents

Celebration Press
Pearson Learning Group

The First Family of Jazz

Imagine growing up in a big family where almost everybody plays music. Your dad plays the piano and your brother plays the trumpet. Three of your other brothers play instruments, too—the saxophone, the trombone, and the drums. Your mom has a beautiful voice and used to sing with a **jazz** band. With a family like that, your house could swing with the sounds of music every night!

The talented Ellis Marsalis at the piano

That's what growing up was like for the Marsalis family of New Orleans. The Marsalis boys spent their childhood playing music with their father, Ellis Marsalis, Jr. He is a jazz pianist and music teacher. He and their mother, Dolores, taught them to work hard to develop their talents. Ellis and Dolores must have been fine teachers, because four of the Marsalis sons grew up to be well-known professional musicians.

Wynton, who is probably the best-known Marsalis, is a world-famous trumpet player. He has won eight **Grammy Awards** for his **classical** and jazz recordings. He also won the 1997 **Pulitzer Prize** for a piece of music he wrote about slavery, called "Blood on the Fields."

Wynton is not the only one in the family to have received a Grammy. His older brother, Branford, who plays the saxophone, has won several Grammy Awards for his jazz and his **pop** recordings. Their brother Delfeayo, who plays the trombone, has also won Grammys for his work as a record producer. It won't be a surprise if Jason, the youngest brother, also wins a Grammy soon. His reputation as a **composer** and drummer is growing fast.

The music of the Marsalis brothers has sparked new excitement about jazz all over America. How did so many musical geniuses grow up in one family?

The Family's Beginnings

Born in 1937, Dolores Ferdinand took piano lessons while she was growing up. She came from a family full of outstanding musicians, including a clarinet player, two trombonists, and a bass player.

Ellis Marsalis, on the other hand, says that his parents did not have any musical ability. Luckily, that did not stop him from developing his musical talents. Born on November 14, 1934, Ellis practiced the cello and the piano as a boy. In college he studied music and began to take a greater interest in piano.

Wynton Marsalis with his mother, Dolores

It wasn't until after college, however, that Ellis was "bitten by the jazz bug," as he puts it. But once he was bitten, he would devote the rest of his life to teaching and playing jazz.

In 1955, after college, Ellis spent a brief period of time on the West Coast playing music. The next year he joined the marines. After a couple of years, he returned to New Orleans, where he married Dolores Ferdinand in 1958. The first two Marsalis sons were Branford, born on August 26, 1960, and Wynton, born on October 18, 1961. The family grew quickly. Ellis III was born in 1964, Delfeayo in 1965, and Mboya in 1970. The last son, Jason, was born in 1977.

While Ellis played piano in New Orleans clubs and taught music, Dolores raised the children. She and Ellis taught their sons to work toward excellence in everything they did. Dolores was a strict disciplinarian who set definite rules for them to follow.

In 1972, Dolores' responsibilities for her children grew. Doctors discovered that Mboya was autistic. This disorder kept him from learning easily or communicating well with others, so Dolores decided to keep Mboya at home and care for him herself. It was a tough job, but with courage and strength, the Marsalis family held together.

The Marsalis family grew so fast that sometimes it was hard for Ellis to make enough money by playing the piano. One day he told Dolores that he thought he should stop playing music. He wanted to get a job as a taxi driver instead. But Dolores knew how much Ellis loved his music, and how sad he would be without it. She encouraged him to continue playing the piano.

Dolores was right to have faith in Ellis. In 1974 he got a teaching job at a new art school called the New Orleans Center for Creative Arts. There he discovered that he loved teaching music to teenagers. Ellis proved himself to be both an amazing jazz pianist *and* an outstanding teacher. Not only did he inspire his sons but also a whole generation of young jazz musicians.

A number of his students, such as Harry Connick, Jr., Terence Blanchard, and Nicholas Payton, became well-known musicians. Today many of them say that Ellis's teaching was an important part of their success. For example, pianist Harry Connick, Jr. said that Ellis changed him into a serious student of music. Because of his influence, Ellis is sometimes called the "patriarch (father) of modern jazz."

Growing Up

When he played jazz in clubs, Ellis brought along his two oldest sons, Branford and Wynton. The boys liked the pop music on the radio better than the jazz they heard in the clubs. Still, they did enjoy being with their dad. "I used to love hanging out with him," Wynton says.

Wynton and Branford had fun with each other, too. Wynton recalls, "We rode our bikes together. We lived in the same room. We both played music."

Branford was five when he began to study music. Ellis tried to teach him to play the piano, but Branford didn't like it and refused to practice. Soon Ellis allowed him to switch to the clarinet, which Branford enjoyed much more. Later he also learned to play the saxophone.

Wynton Marsalis enjoys spending time with his father, Ellis.

7

Wynton was five when he began taking music lessons from his father. When he was six, he got his first trumpet as a gift from his father's friend, the famous trumpeter Al Hirt.

At first Wynton was not very good at playing the trumpet. When his father's friends heard him play, they would ask, "Are you sure you're Ellis's son?"

When Wynton was eight or nine, he played in the Fairview Baptist Church marching band, conducted by Danny Barker. The band played at the first New Orleans Jazz and Heritage Festival. Wynton admitted later that he did not play the trumpet well that day.

However, Wynton is a motivated person. He wants to be the best at whatever he does, including playing the trumpet. So when he was 12 or 13, he began to spend hours practicing every day. He kept up that habit during the following years of his life, and his ability developed quickly.

With their parents' encouragement, Wynton and Branford took private lessons, went to music camps and festivals, and played with marching bands. The Marsalis family did not have much money, so the boys had to earn scholarships to pay for their music training. They practiced so much that by the time they were teenagers, they were both excellent musicians.

Branford and Wynton

Branford loved pop music best of all. When he was still in high school, he started a **funk** music group called The Creators. Ellis Marsalis encouraged his son Wynton to join the group, too.

Wynton and Branford loved working together on their music and had a special energy when they played together. The Creators became a popular local band. Wynton and Branford began to earn money from playing music at clubs and dances. Such jobs are called "gigs."

Wynton (left) and Branford have always enjoyed playing together.

Although he enjoyed playing music with his brother, Wynton was not as interested in pop music as Branford was. Instead, he liked jazz, the swinging American music he had listened to while he was growing up. He also loved European classical music, especially the trumpet playing of the famous French musician Maurice André.

Growing up African American in racially mixed New Orleans was not always easy for the Marsalis boys. As Wynton grew more interested in classical music, he worried that he might encounter hurtful racism if he tried to become a classical musician. African American musicians created jazz music, and many great jazz musicians are African American. However, there were not many African American classical musicians. Wynton wondered how well he would fit into the world of classical music, but he also knew that he loved it too much to stay away. "I had to succumb [give in] to the greatness of the music," he said.

When he was in tenth grade, Wynton entered a classical **concerto** competition and won. Before long he was playing in classical concerts with the New Orleans Philharmonic Symphony and the New Orleans Civic Orchestra—even though he was only in high school!

The Marsalis family was very close. As Branford remembers, "We didn't have the kind of house where, as a 15-year-old kid, you would lock your door and put a *Keep Out* sign on it. . . . Forget it. We were a family and we all lived together."

But as the boys grew older, the time came to leave home. Wynton was only 17 when he traveled to New York City for an **audition** at the Juilliard School, one of the best music and performing arts schools in the world. Wynton did not have a suitcase, so he packed his things into a cardboard box for the trip.

The famous Juilliard School in New York City

Many young musicians want to study music at Juilliard, but only a few of the very best students are accepted. In 1979, Wynton passed his Juilliard audition easily and won a four-year scholarship.

While he was at Juilliard for his audition, Wynton saw an announcement of tryouts for the Tanglewood Music Festival in Lenox, Massachusetts. If he could get in, he would be able to spend that summer playing music with excellent classical musicians. He decided to try out.

For his Tanglewood audition, Wynton played parts of a concerto by Johann Sebastian Bach. This music is so difficult that few professional trumpeters can play it without making a mistake. Wynton played it flawlessly. Even though Tanglewood ordinarily did not admit students under 18, Wynton was eagerly accepted. Gunther Schuller was president of the New England Conservatory and one of the judges who decided which students to accept. He said of Wynton, "If he was three and a half, I would take him." He called Wynton "a beautiful, young, fresh talent."

At Tanglewood that summer, Wynton practiced so hard that sometimes he woke the other students up in the middle of the night. That fall, he began his studies at Juilliard.

While Wynton was training at Juilliard, Branford was in Boston, studying mostly the alto saxophone at another famous school, the Berklee College of Music. He liked to visit Wynton in New York, where the brothers would play jazz with other young musicians. Branford and Wynton learned a great deal about music from their studies, from the musicians they met, and from their gigs at concerts and clubs.

By this time the music world was beginning to notice the remarkable talents of the Marsalis brothers.

Branford Marsalis plays a swinging alto sax.

Wynton couldn't pass up the opportunity to join the Jazz Messengers, led by drummer Art Blakey.

In 1980, Wynton had a thrilling opportunity— Art Blakey, the famous jazz musician, asked Wynton to join his group, the Jazz Messengers.

Unfortunately, joining the Jazz Messengers meant leaving Juilliard. Wynton still loved the classical music he was studying in school, but he also wanted to become a serious jazz musician.

Wynton called his father to ask for advice. "I always talked to my daddy to see what he was thinking," he explained later. Even before he asked, Wynton knew that his father would tell him to join Blakey's group. "Some people think you should take the safe road. He's not like that. His idea is, go out there and do it. If you fail it, you tried it. Don't stay at home. Don't be afraid."

Musical Success

Wynton joined Art Blakey's band and toured the world playing jazz. He made his first recordings with the Jazz Messengers. In 1981, Branford also joined the group. Once again the Marsalis brothers were playing together.

Art Blakey encouraged Wynton to compose his own music and, eventually, to form his own band. By 1982, Wynton had his own group, and Branford joined him. They found a drummer, a pianist, and other musicians and toured the United States, Europe, and Japan.

In the 1980s many people liked listening to "fusion jazz," which is played by blending electronic instruments and **acoustic instruments**. But Wynton liked acoustic jazz better. As his career grew, he helped make acoustic jazz more popular.

By this time Wynton was gaining fame for his jazz recordings. In 1981 his first album was nominated for a Grammy Award. It did not win, but in 1983 his second album, *Think of One*, did. Because of Wynton's success, a new generation of musicians was becoming interested in acoustic jazz.

Wynton enjoyed performing both jazz and classical music. When he began making records, some people suggested that he should concentrate on one kind of music or the other. It is very difficult to excel at playing either one of these styles of music, so most performers do not try to do both.

Wynton Marsalis is different, however. He kept on playing and recording both jazz and classical music. In 1983 he won two Grammy Awards—one for his **solo** performance on a jazz recording and the other for his solo performance on a classical recording. The next year he won two Grammys again in the same categories!

Wynton holds the Grammy he won in 1984 for best jazz solo instrumental performance.

Branford was still playing jazz, but he continued to be interested in popular music, too. In 1985, when he was 25, he left Wynton's group to play pop rock with the international star Sting. Later he also played with pop artists like the Grateful Dead and Bruce Hornsby.

Throughout his career Branford has continued to enjoy popular music, but he has become a successful jazz musician, too. He won a Grammy in 1993 for one of his jazz albums, *I Heard You Twice the First Time*. He was also honored for his pop music with a Grammy in 1994 for "Barcelona Mona," recorded with Bruce Hornsby for the Olympics in Spain. With his group Buckshot LeFonque, Branford plays in still another style, blending the sounds of jazz and **hip-hop**.

In addition, Branford worked in television for several years as the musical director of *The Tonight Show*. He has also had an acting career, appearing in several movies. Branford continues to record and perform both jazz and popular music. He has taught in the jazz studies department at Michigan State University. He has also worked as a creative consultant for Columbia Records, helping them find talented new musicians.

In his 20s, Wynton's fame as a musician grew rapidly. He made many jazz and classical recordings, performed all over the world, and became an international jazz star.

In 1987, Wynton became the artistic director of Classical Jazz, a program that brings jazz performances to Lincoln Center in New York City. He has won two Peabody Awards—a broadcasting award for excellence—for his video series *Marsalis on Music* and for a 26-part radio series on jazz called *Making the Music*. He also played a central role in Ken Burns's television documentary *Jazz*.

Wynton is a top-level performer who has been called "potentially the greatest classical trumpeter of all time." Still, playing the trumpet is not his only goal.

Perhaps because he grew up watching his father teach, Wynton cares deeply about music education. He loves to visit schools to teach children about music, especially the trumpet and jazz. In his video series *Marsalis on Music*, he dribbles a basketball to demonstrate rhythm and makes up a tale about a hamster that got loose, to show how music uses dramatic themes. Wynton also began a concert series at Lincoln Center called *Jazz for Young People,* with talks on topics like "What Is Swing?" and "Who Is Louis Armstrong?"

The Rest of the Family

Meanwhile back in New Orleans the younger Marsalis brothers were growing up and developing their own careers. Just like Wynton and Branford, Ellis III and Delfeayo grew up as a pair, attending the same schools and doing everything together. As a boy, Ellis III liked sports and writing poetry. He played the guitar a little, but he was never serious about music. He joined the military and later studied business and history. Eventually he went to work running his own computer business.

Jason (left) and Delfeayo Marsalis spent a lot of time together while growing up.

Delfeayo chose the trombone as his instrument when he was in sixth grade. He is interested in jazz and "**avant garde**," or modern, music. As an adult he composes jazz musicals, leads his own band, and has played his trombone with famous jazz artists like Ray Charles, Art Blakey, and Fats Domino. He also likes to write stories.

Delfeayo is even better known as a producer. As the person in charge of the recording session, a producer makes edits and determines the final sound of the recording. Delfeayo produced his first recording—his father's album *Syndrome*—when he was just 17. Since then he has produced more than 70 recordings, including works by his father and brothers as well as other jazz artists. Four of the recordings have won Grammy Awards.

Delfeayo Marsalis, the family's trombone player

Jason, the youngest Marsalis, is gaining recognition as a brilliant drummer and composer. When he was three, his mother and father gave him a toy drum set. Jason loved to bang on it. In school he learned to play the violin, but he didn't forget about his drum set. Before long he switched from the violin to the drums.

Jason grew up to play drums with a band called Los Hombres Calientes and with other musicians. He has made his own albums, written a musical, and worked with his father and his older brothers on recordings. One of his albums, *Music in Motion*, includes only Jason's own compositions.

Like his famous sons, Ellis Marsalis, Jr., has had a remarkable musical career. He has made many important jazz recordings, and he is one of the leading jazz educators in America. He is the head of the Jazz Studies program at the University of New Orleans and continues to perform as a jazz pianist.

Ellis believes that all schools should teach students how music is related to other academic subjects. He told a reporter, "Personally, I don't see how anyone can teach history without teaching the arts. What you get then is just dead presidents and war heroes."

An Amazing Family

What has made the Marsalis family so successful? The Marsalis sons would probably say it was partly hard work and partly the result of growing up with parents who love music. Music has always been a part of their lives. Wynton said, "My daddy played all the time and we all looked up to him."

Branford explained that it was his parents' attitude about hard work that also guided them toward success. "It wasn't the kind of family where my parents said you have to make the honor roll or you're a failure. They said you have to do the best you can do, or you're a failure."

Wynton dribbles a basketball to teach rhythm to young people.

Wynton gave some excellent advice to young musicians in an interview with *Highlights for Children* magazine. "Practice," he said. "It's important to practice on your own, but it's also important to get around other musicians and share information about music. Participate in musical ensembles, go hear professional musicians play—just become interested and active in learning about the music."

The Marsalis brothers are super-talented musicians. But that doesn't mean that they were always good at everything. At first Wynton played the trumpet badly. Sometimes Branford got poor grades. To other people these might be embarrassing failures. But Ellis and Dolores Marsalis taught their sons a different lesson. The Marsalis family knows that a person who wants to succeed also has to be willing to risk failure.

Here is Wynton's advice to anyone who is trying to succeed at a difficult task. "You never know when you're going to fail," he said. "That's just a part of succeeding—failing. And it's not that big a deal. It's something to laugh about." If you do fail at something, Wynton adds, just pick yourself up and try again. "That's how you succeed."

Glossary

acoustic instuments instruments that are not electrically amplified

audition a tryout for a performer

avant garde modern styles of art or music that explore new ideas and approaches

classical referring to music that emphasizes formal composition and requires training to perform, such as symphonies, concertos, and operas

composer a writer of music

concerto a long musical composition played by one or more solo instruments with an orchestra

funk an African-influenced blend of soul music and rock, popular in the 1970s

Grammy Awards annual awards given by the National Academy of Recording Arts and Sciences for musical recordings made in the United States

hip-hop music created by scratching (turning a vinyl record by hand), sampling (using parts of existing songs to create new music), and rapping (rhythmic chanting of spoken words)

jazz a kind of American music developed by African Americans in the early 1900s. It has strong rhythms and accents at unusual places.

pop entertaining music influenced by rock and jazz, and produced for a large audience

Pulitzer Prize annual award given for outstanding achievement in literature, music, and journalism

solo a musical piece played or sung by a single musician